A SWING FOR A LIFETIME

By Michael Callahan

Printed in The United States of America

ISBN: 978-0-9978317-6-4

A Swing For a Lifetime /Callahan-1st ed.

1. Golf,. 2. Golf Instruction. 3. Sports. 4. Callahan

NFB/Amelia Press
<<◇>>
119 Dorchester Road
Buffalo, New York 14213
For more information please visit
nfbpublishing.com

To a very special woman who came back into my life to learn how to play golf, and ended up giving me the inspiration to finish this body of work. In the process of this, she became the love of my life. To her I thank from the bottom of my heart. I love you very much.

A Swing For a Lifetime

TABLE OF CONTENTS

INTRODUCTION

Let me start by saying that all golf swings work. How is that possible? Golf swings with poor fundamentals only work to a point. How they work is through compensation in the swing but they lack consistency as far as direction, ball flight, distance, etc.

Over the years, I have found that amateurs who have poor fundamentals tend to make their swing work, but have a tendency to play inconsistently. All the students I have taught seem to have one recurring concern. Everyone wants to be consistent in all parts of his or her game. A player with poor fundamentals must make one or more compensations in order to make his or her swing work. Making compensations in your golf swing can lead to many inconsistencies such as inconsistent scoring, direction and flight of the ball and or poor balance.

This book is about the golf swing and how to keep it simple. The key to good golf is simplicity and the rest is psychological. The swing itself is very simple to understand, but the execution of the swing can be difficult without proper fundamentals. Since it is based on the laws of physics and geometry, one needs to learn some of these basic principles. As long as you do not violate one of these laws, the ball will travel to its intended target. It is when one of these laws is violated where one will need to make some type of compensation in the swing to get the ball close to its intended target. Therefore, you will need to make the necessary adjustment in your downswing, which is instinctive.

Throughout this book, I'll talk about the positive aspects of the swing, as well as the common swing flaws that I have come across while teaching students. There are also many misconceptions of the golf swing that I will clear up. I feel it is important to understand the basic fundamentals of the swing and some common swing flaws in order to know what you are trying to accomplish. You must be able to differentiate between what a proper swing and a poor swing feel like. Once you have an understanding of these differences, you will then be able to make the necessary adjustments to correct the flaws in your swing. You must remember old habits die hard. Even after you have corrected your swing flaws, old habits can creep back into your swing after a period of time, even years later. Without consistent practice and reinforcement of good habits it will be difficult to improve your golf swing. Therefore, it is always beneficial to keep notes or a journal on drills or lessons you may have taken to correct your flaws for future reference. I myself have a journal that goes back many years now plus video tapes of lessons and practice sessions that I refer back to when necessary. This helps to reinforce what I have learned.

One area of golf that hasn't been written enough about, until recent years, is the mental aspect of golf or golf psychology. In this chapter, I'll talk about the thinking process using visualization instead of verbal communication or words to execute the golf swing. Playing target golf on the course verses mechanical swing golf will also be covered.

While reading this book, you must remember that it is one thing to understand the golf swing, but quite another to actually feel how a proper swing feels like with good, sound fundamentals. Through the use of drills, you will gain a better understanding of what a good swing feels like. While doing the drills in this book, it is important to remember that you do not go full speed or try to hit the ball for distance. Do the drills slowly or in slow motion at first. You want to make contact with the ball, but don't try to swing a full speed to get distance. This will give you a better feel as to where the club is going and how the body is moving through the golf swing. It also gives the muscles time to remember what they did so they can repeat this motion. Also, you want to hit the ball during the drills, but do not try to steer or manipulate the club to hit the ball. Let the ball just get in the way of the club.

CHAPTER 1: TYPES OF RELEASES

There are a few ways to release the club in the golf swing. The first is using the hands. A body release type swing is the second type.

A hands release method has been used by many golfers and taught by many golf professionals for decades. It is still taught today. Many golfers who use this type of release have many inconsistencies. I, myself, was taught this type of release as a child, but knew in my late teens of the inconsistencies with it, especially in scoring and high pressure situations. The release tends to break down very easily and prevents you from scoring well.

With today's technology and the use of video cameras, computer video and launch monitors, slow motion can be used to show students exactly where their swing flaws are and how these flaws affect the direction and flight path of the golf ball.

In a hands release, the hands and arms control the club and

release it. How is this done? This can be accomplished in three different ways with different results.

The way it is taught is to have your hands flip or rotate your right hand over the left hand as you swing through the impact zone allowing the clubface to square off. The problem with this type of release is that the timing of your hands has got to be absolutely perfect every time in order for the ball to fly to its intended target. If your timing happens to be off, you can see a lot of the golf course, even parts you may have never seen or thought existed. This will increase your score, especially if there is a hazard or out of bounds on the hole. With a hands release, when you miss hit the ball, that ball tends to be anywhere from a little to a lot off target. It all depends on how much the timing of your hands are off at impact.

Another common fault with this type of release is that golfers tend to have a lot of lateral movement before hitting the golf ball. Many of us have heard the term leg drive before. What exactly is it? It is one of the many misconceptions of what truly happens with the legs in the golf swing. Leg drive is just like it sounds. It is using the legs to push or drive through as we swing the club through the ball. As a result of this, the right elbow reacts by pulling into the right side of the body and the right shoulder drops down increasing the steepness of the shoulders. As this happens, you must rely on the hands to square off the club at impact by rotating them. If the hands fail to rotate, the clubface will remain open and the ball will end up right of your target. The amount of power lost due to using the hands is about 50%. This is because the right elbow is pulled into the side and becomes trapped. As a result of this, the club will start to decelerate as it approaches the ball. You can still generate enough power to get distance, but it will be hard to be accurate the majority of the time. My friend always said he would much rather hit it straight and short than long and crooked. It is easier to play and score better and makes the game more enjoyable.

A third fault of a hands release is the lack of body rotation through the ball. The majority of the time it is because the legs were driven through the ball or the hips moved laterally. When this happens, the upper body can no longer rotate because it doesn't have the legs in a position to support it so it can rotate. In order for the shoulders and hips to rotate properly, the right leg needs to react to the hips rotating and move as the hips move rotationally. I'll talk more on this later in the body rotation chapter.

What is a body release? A body release is where the bigger muscles in the body do the work and control the swing. The bigger muscles are the shoulders, chest, and back. Hitting the ball is less work when the upper body is in control of the smaller muscles (hands and arms). This will help to improve poor shots. An example would be to take a look at two different car engines from different times. If we looked at a car engine from the 1960s, we would find the engine has a lot of moving parts. We can also expect the engine to break down and need repairs after 10,000 to 20,000 miles. We would also have to tune it up frequently. Now let's look at an engine built more recently like this year. Today, there are a lot less moving parts in the engine, fewer break downs, tune-ups are done less frequently and engines are lasting much longer compared to those of the 1960s. How does this example compare to the golf swing? The simpler you keep the swing and the fewer moving parts you have, allows for a more sound and consistent swing. Going about making some changes may not be as difficult as you may think. It all depends on where your swing is at and how good are your fundamentals. Any time you make changes to your golf swing; it takes time for them to become habits. For example, if you make one swing change it generally takes about three weeks for you to get used to the change. But it will take three months for that one change to become a habit. If you're making three or changes, it will take much longer.

While teaching students and getting their swings back on track, I'll only pick out one or two changes that need to be made during a lesson. The reason for this is so the student can focus on the one change and not be able to think about three or four things at once. When more than one swing thought occurs, many students tend to send mixed signals to their muscles by using the left side of the brain. I'll talk more about this in chapter 9.

By allowing the body to control the arms and club, our miss hits will improve and tend not to be in another fairway. Simply put, miss hits should not be so far to the left or right of our intended target. Eventually our miss hits should be approximately ten to fifteen yards to the left or right of the target at most. This gives you about a twenty to thirty yard margin for error. To have miss-hits that close to the target takes time, practice and a lot of patience. Every once in a while you may still hit a really bad shot that is well off target. Even the tour pros hit really poor shots once in a while but their misses are still in a good spot, either on the fairway or just in the first cut of rough. They also practice a lot more than the average golfer. I can help you to improve your golf swing to make the game more enjoyable. It is up to you to put the time and practice in to achieve you goals.

CHAPTER 2: THE GRIP

In order to have a good sound golf swing, one must first know how to grip the club properly. I like to teach the grip a number of different ways depending on the level of golfer I am working with. With beginners, I like to teach the grip through the use of a yardstick. Take the yardstick and grip it naturally in both hands. Examine your grip on the yardstick. You should find that the grip will be more in the fingers and that the palms of your hands will probably be facing each other. This is how the hands should be on the club. The palms should face each other so that the wrists can make the proper hinging motion during the backswing. It is a lot easier to get the grip right on a yardstick because a a yardstick is flat. The palms face each other right of the bat. Remember, it's very important that the palms face each other so the wrists can hinge properly. The golf shaft and grip are round which makes it harder to get the hands on the club properly.

Another way I teach the golf grip is to have students take

the club by the clubhead and lay the shaft, not the grip, across the left hand. Next, set the shaft at a diagonal across your left hand so that it runs through the first knuckle of your index finger and the base of the palm. Now close the hand so that the right pad of your left hand sits on top of the shaft. The thumb should point down the right center of the shaft and be close to the index finger. You should be able to see two to two and a half knuckles of your left hand. I find that many students tend to grip the club either too much in the fingers or too much in the palm of their hand.

When you go to grip the club on the proper end, you should check to see if it's right. To do this, grip the club in your left hand only. Now take your last three fingers off the club, leaving your index finger and thumb on the club. The club should not have move at all and will be balanced. If it has, re-grip the club and check to make sure the club is running diagonally across your hand as you did earlier. Lastly take your thumb off. The club should not have moved and should be balanced in your hand. Now the grip in your left hand is correct. The main thing I look for is to have the club in a balanced and square position. You'll also find that the grip pressure needed to hold the club is minimal.

With the right hand, you want to lay the shaft in between

the first two knuckles of your middle fingers. The index finger will wrap around the shaft and act more like a trigger finger. It should feel as if you are going to pull the trigger of a gun. From here, close your hand so that the gap between the two pads cover and hide the thumb of your left hand. The thumb of your right hand should point down the left center of the shaft.

The reason I have you grip the club on the shaft first is because it is much easier to FEEL where the shaft runs through the hand than by gripping at the grip end. Now take your grip at the grip end of the club. You should be able to hinge your wrists very easily. If you can't, start at the beginning and grip the club again.

For those of you who have a strong left hand grip and would like to have a more neutral grip, I'll give you another drill to help. Take the club in your right hand and hold it in front of you so that the shaft is vertical and the toe of the club is facing you. Now put your left hand on the club like you are going to shake hands with someone. From here, slide your right hand down the shaft until the hands meet. Close your right hand and allow the thumb of your left hand to fit in between the gap in the palm of the right hand.

It is very important to get the palms of the hands to match each other. To see this put your palms together so they face each other. Now move your right hand above the left. The only thing left is to tilt both hands to the right a little bit and make a fist. There's your golf grip in a nutshell. There are many other ways I teach the correct grip. These are just a few simple ways.

CHAPTER 3: POSTURE AND ALIGNMENT

Building a sound golf swing is similar to building a sturdy house. In building a house, there must be a solid foundation for the house to stay up under different weather conditions. The same is true to building a sound golf swing. There must be a solid foundation. The next step is learning the posture and the alignment of our body and clubface.

As a golf instructor, the first things I look at in a student's swing are their posture, body alignment and ball position. These are the three recurring faults, other than the grip, in the golf swing I find in many amateurs. In some lessons, a simple change as ball position, for example, can change or correct the direction of the ball if the golfer has good fundamentals.

The posture is very, very, critical to the golf swing. If this should be even slightly off, the results can be disastrous. How do we set up to the ball? Most students I have taught, whether beginner or low handicapper, get to the right stadium but the wrong seat. They all seem to bend from the waist. Bending from the waist causes the spine angle to be curved and puts the pelvis in a poor position for the hips to rotate properly. Also, the range of motion in the hips is limited to how little they will turn.

What is a spine angle? A spine angle is the angle the spine takes in the setup. It must be kept as flat as possible and not too rounded. When the student's back has a rounded look to it, I first start to look at the position of the student's pelvis and shoulders. You may be wondering what the pelvis has to do with a rounded back or the spine angle. I look to see if the pelvis is pushed inward towards the ball. In this position, the lower back has a rounded look to it and the student would not feel the lower back muscle tighten. By allowing the pelvis to be pushed in, the hips are limited in the amount they can rotate. Also, the lower back muscles will tend to stretch the wrong way and will not create a coil or tension on the backswing to help generate power. This can cause lower back pain. If the pelvis is pushed inward, the back will have a very rounded and slouched look to it.

To set up to the ball properly, you must stand straight and bend from the pelvis NOT the waist. As you bend over, keep your legs locked and your spine fairly flat. It is okay if the upper back is a little rounded as long as the shoulders re not slouched. My main concern is getting the pelvis and lower back in a good position for the body to move right. This will allow the hips to have a good range of motion. From here, bend your knees only a little bit and keep your rear end out. It should feel as though you are going to sit in the edge of a barstool.

To see if your posture is correct, you'll need a full-length mirror and a yardstick. Get back into your posture in front of the mirror. Make sure you are standing so that your right side is facing the mirror. Next hang the yardstick so that it hangs through the back center of your shoulder. It should pass through the reference points of the back center of the shoulders, butt end of the club in your hand, the front of the knees and the balls of your feet. See figure 1 on the next page.

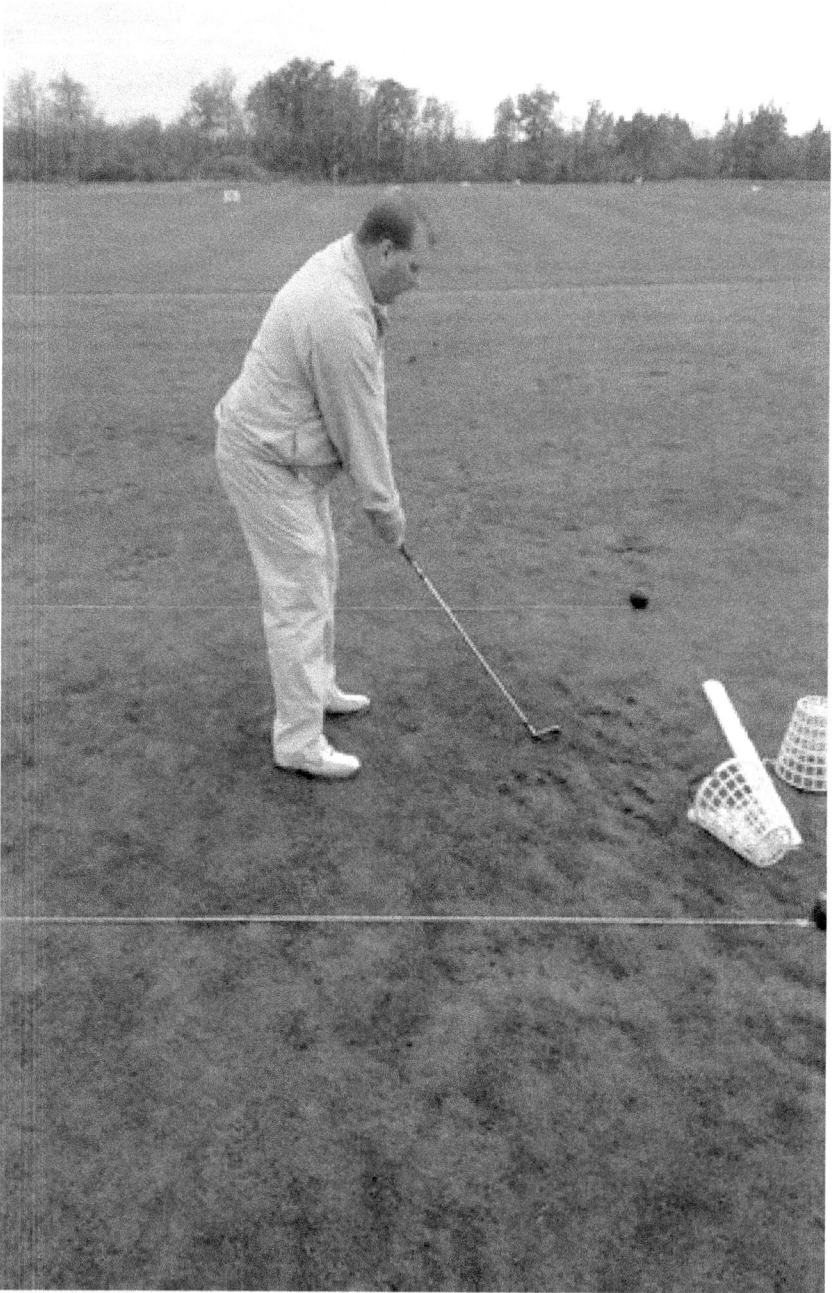

Figure 1

The last part of getting into the correct posture is tilting the spine. From the waist up, you want to tilt the upper body (or spine) to the right if you are right handed golfer about 5 degrees or so. When looking in a mirror from the side view, the hips should be level. The shoulders will be tilted and should also be parallel to the eyes. See figure 2 on the next page.

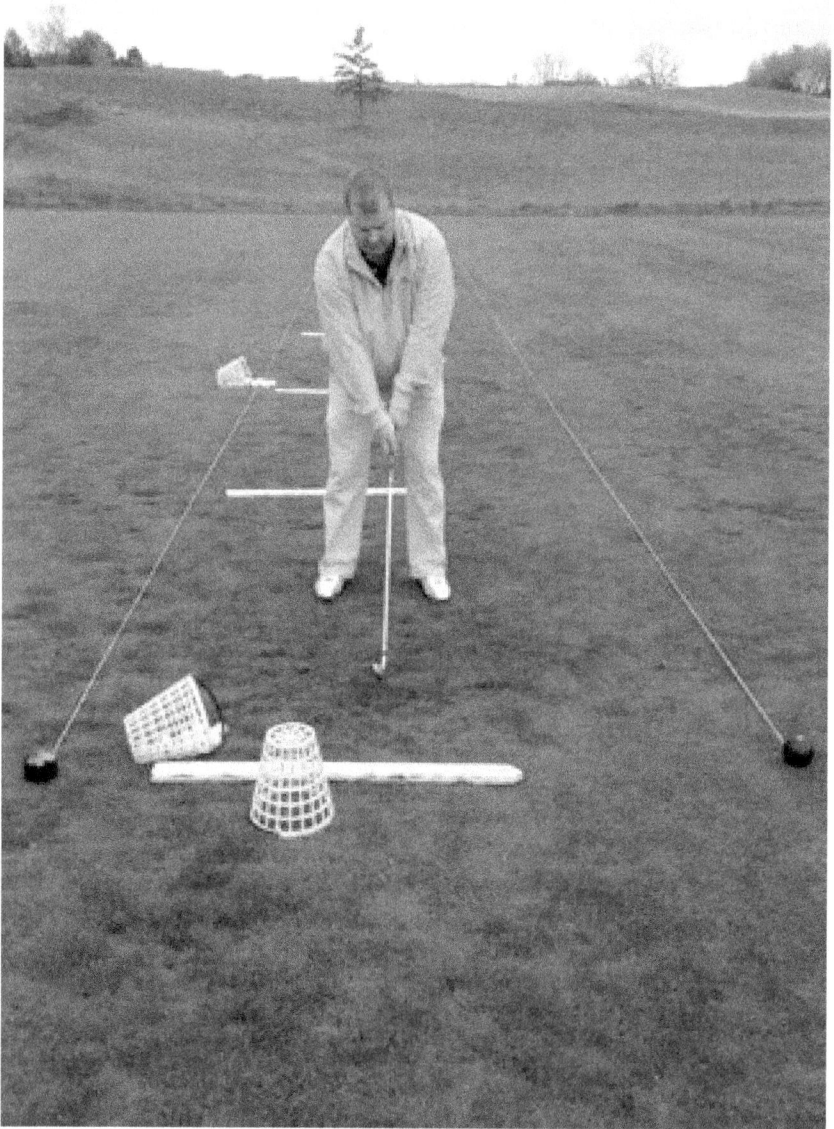

Figure 2

Once your posture is correct, you need to learn how to align your body up so you can get the ball to its intended target. This is called alignment. If your alignment is off, the ball will probably not get to its intended target without some type of compensation in the swing or lots of luck. One of the biggest flaws I see students make is aligning their body up with their intended target. If you align your body up to your intended target, one of two things will tend to happen. First, the clubface could be aimed at the target, and the body will also be aimed at the target. This puts the body in a closed position and could cause you to hit a draw or big hook.

So how does one insure proper setup? The easiest way to learn alignment is to take two yardsticks or golf clubs, either will work. Lay them down so they are parallel to each other and about two feet apart. Place the ball between the yardsticks and take your stance next to the left yardstick making sure your feet are parallel to them and the same distance from the yardsticks. Next, check to make sure your shoulders, chest, hips, thighs and feet are all parallel to the yardsticks. If not, go through the above steps again.

One of the more common faults students make with their

alignment is the tendency to get everything in alignment except for the shoulders. They are usually left opened and aimed left of the target. It is very important that the shoulders are aligned properly with the rest of the body. A miscue here could result in hitting the ball off line.

How about foot positioning? Like I said earlier, you want the feet to be parallel to your target, but should they be turned in, out or perpendicular to the yardstick. It's simple. Point your left foot out towards the target between 15 to 25 degrees. This will help to promote a good hip turn and improve balance. If your feet are positioned perpendicular to the shafts at your feet, your hips have a better chance of moving laterally or sliding.

The final preparation to make is ball position. The ball should be placed forward of the center of your stance with the shorter clubs and moved further forward as the club gets longer. The driver should be placed on the heel of your left foot or even slightly more forward. To help give you a better visual of the ball position, take a yardstick and place it perpendicular to the other to yardsticks used to get yourself lined up to the target. Why is the ball placed so far forward? This is where the club actually squares itself off. As the clubs get longer, the club will square up further forward in your stance because of its length. Many golfers have learned to place the ball further back in their stance with the short irons. There's nothing wrong with playing the ball back, but the majority of golfers who do this, do it for the wrong reason. For example, some golfers believe that placing the ball back in their stance will put more backspin on the ball to hold the green. Not so. What actually happens is you are de-lofting the club, causing the ball flight to be in a lower trajectory. For example, a nine iron turns into say a seven iron depending on how far back the ball position is. This is a good shot to hit if you're hitting into a strong wind or need to keep the ball low to fly underneath a tree limb.

CHAPTER 4: BODY ROTATION

What role does the body take in the golf swing? How does it move? What is in control of the golf club? Where does the power come from? These are just a few of the questions students ask me on a regular basis. There are many, many others.

To answer these questions and others that have been or will be asked, we must start with understanding the body's role in the golf swing. Everything in the golf swing is related to your core muscles. Your upper body reacts to it and your lower body reacts to it. How does this occur? First, you need to understand what your core muscles are. Your core muscles are your abs, stomach, lower back and hips.

What is the first move in the golf swing or how does it start? There are many different answers you can get. The first part of the body that moves or starts the golf swing are the hips, not the arms or hands or legs. The right hip should turn right from the start and stay either on or inside the right heel though the top of the back swing. As this happens, the upper body will react and turn with the hips and momentum should allow the upper body to finish a complete turn.

The upper body's role is to turn or rotate around the spine during the backswing and the downswing. It is this motion by which the club is moved back and through the ball.

Where does the power in the swing come from? There are many areas power comes from but I do not want to get technical and want to keep things simple. I usually talk to students about 3 main sources of power.

The first area of power comes from the rotation of the body. This is where the power starts to generate. The upper body rotates on top of the legs. You want the legs to move as little as possible but allow them to give a little. This creates a coil effect of the upper body. To give you an example of this, take a toy top and wrap the cord around it tight. When you pull the cord, the top spins very fast. It also stays upright for a bit. Now if you take the toy top and wrap the cord around it loosely, it spins slower and wobbles. Apply this same theory to the golf swing. Rotate the upper body and try to keeps the legs quiet but allow them to give a little. As the upper body unwinds, it unwinds quickly. This in turn will give the clubhead speed without you trying to create it. Now if you allow the legs to move a lot in the rotation of the backswing, the upper body unwinds slowly and sluggishly. Also, the hips may not rotate and instead slide or move laterally. This will cause many other problems in the swing.

The drill I give students the most often to understand and feel body rotation and coil is to take a long bar or your driver and put it over the back of your shoulders with your arms extended along the bar or at the ends of the driver. Take your golf posture and turn or rotate your shoulders without moving your legs, but allow them to give slightly. You should feel pressure or tension in the sides of your body. The tension you feel is called coil. The tighter the coiling of the upper body, the faster it will uncoil on the downswing. This is where the speed of the club is generated from. As a result, there is no need to try and create speed with the arms. Instead speed of the arms and club are generated. If you start trying to create the speed with the arms, the upper body will not be able to keep up and stay in control. As a result of creating speed, the clubface will be in an open position at impact unless you get the hands to rotate or flip over to square the clubface at impact. This technique is a hands release.

A common flaw I find students make in this drill above is they allow the right leg to straighten and the knee turns outward. It's very important to maintain the flex in the right knee. Try to keep the right knee inside of the right foot on the backswing. When the right leg straightens, the upper body does not have a very tight coil to it. Therefore, you will lose some power.

Another common flaw made is the tendency to move laterally with the hips. Although there is some lateral movement, it is very minimal and cannot be felt. Concentrate more on rotating the shoulders and chest around your spine. If you do this drill in front of a mirror, you will be able to see if any of the previously mentioned flaws occur. You can also use a video camera if you have access to one.

Actual clubhead speed starts from the upper body and is projected outwards. To understand how the speed is projected outwards in the swing, I'll give you a visual image and illustration. Take four circles. Each one bigger than the next and put them inside each other. Now draw a straight line from the smallest circle through the middle circle and then to the outer circles. Where am I going with this? It is very simple geometry that applies to the golf swing. If you were to move the smallest circle where the line connects, the other three circles will also move. As you increase the speed of the smallest circle, the middle circle will move even faster than the smaller circle, and the outside circles will move even faster than both other circles because it has a greater distance to travel. Keep in mind, that it is the inner circle that is controlling the speed. It would be the same as watching a bicycle tire rolling. The inside of the axle is always moving slower than the outside of the tire.

If you apply this theory to the golf swing, the small circle represents the hips. The next smallest circle represents the shoulders. The next size circle represents the hands while the biggest circle represents the club head. Another drill I like to give students to see and feel this is to hold a book with both hands. Place your hands on opposite sides of the book. Get into your golf posture. Next bend your elbows so the book is in front of your body. Now rotate your hips and shoulders. As you do this, allow the arms to move and keep the book in front of you. Rotate in the opposite direction allowing the arms to move with book. This is how the club moves in the golf swing. The bigger muscles of the body (abs, chest, and back) move and control the arms and club.

Chapter 5: Position One – The Takeaway

As I said earlier, the golf swing itself is very simple. It is the execution that is hard because of how we think. Our brains can get in the way and we over think. This I will get into in a later chapter.

I break the swing down in to four parts, which consist of the takeaway, top of the swing, impact and the follow through. In this chapter, I will talk about the takeaway. Any position I talk about is only a REFERENCE point and not an exact position. A position like 8 o'clock for one person, maybe closer to 7 or 9 o'clock for another.

With the aid of a mirror or video camera, you can see your club and body pass through the reference points I will be talking about. When using a camera or mirror, there are two angles you look at. The first angle is from the front facing the mirror. The second is from the back to see the swing path, swing plane spine angle, etc.

To best see the swing in a static mode, or while walking through the swing slowly, I recommend using a full length mirror. Using a mirror will give you instant feedback while walking through the swing to get a visual image in your mind of where the club and body are going and also check to see if you go through the proper reference points. Take your golf posture and use the mirror to check it. To start the takeaway, rotate your right hip and allow your shoulders, arms and club to follow the movement of your upper body. The hips, shoulders, arms and club must move together as one unit. The right hip should stay inside the right heel. The hip should not have any lateral motion and should not end up outside of the right heel. You may feel like the right hip is moving towards your left heel. If you look in the mirror from face on, you should see the right hip inside of the right heel. The hip should not be in the center of your stance though. See figure 1 and 2 on the following pages

Figure 1

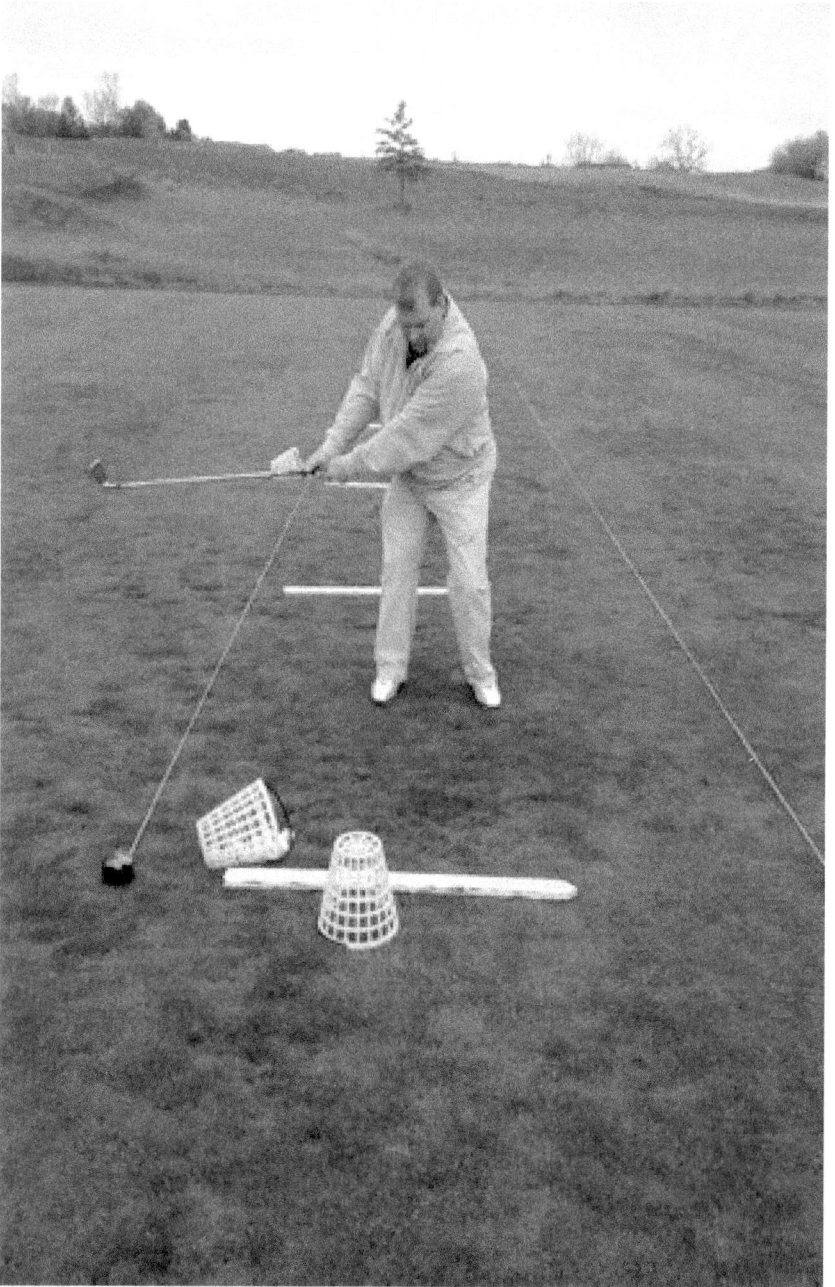

Figure 2

Before you start to take the club up, stop the takeaway. When the arms and club approach eight o'clock, stop and hold this position for ten seconds. The reason for this pause is to give your muscles a chance to remember where they are moving. A drill I use often with beginners is I have them put the butt end of the club in their navel and stretch the arms out down the shaft until they form a triangle. Now turn the hips. As you can see, the shoulders, arms, hands and club move together as the hips start the takeaway. This is how they work as a unit. This drill will help you learn how the body controls the motion of your hands and arms in the takeaway.

What about the lower body during the takeaway? Do the legs move? If so, how or how much do they move? These are some of the frequent questions I am often asked. The movement of the legs in the takeaway is very minimal. You should keep the legs fairly quiet. The left leg should move inwards toward the ball only a smidge as a result of the hips. The less you allow the left leg to move the better off you will be. The legs are used primarily as a base of support for the upper body to rotate on top. of and used for resistance to create a coiling of the upper body, which I mentioned earlier in chapter four.

Once you have gotten into the takeaway and are at the

eight o'clock point, check to see if you are in the proper position. The clubhead should appear to be in a slightly closed position. This is only an optical illusion from your point of view. The clubhead is actually square to the swing path. If it's not, you may have rotated the left forearm up, which will open clubface. In this case the clubface will be vertical to the ground or could be facing skyward depending on how much the left forearm has rotated. Now the leading edge of the clubface will face to the left.

If the clubface is facing the ground, then you have rotated the left forearm down. The rotation of the left forearm is the most common fault I see in and through the takeaway. To give you an example of what it feels like, simply put the club in your left hand only and hold the club parallel to the ground in front of you. Now turn your left forearm to the right. This is what many students do in the takeaway and as a result the clubface opens up. It is important for you to understand what this motion feels like. Once you can feel this forearm rotation, you can then begin to differentiate between right way and wrong way. Since you have rotated the left forearm going back, you'll have to rotate it in the opposite direction on the way down and through the ball in order for the clubface to be squared off. If the left forearm does not rotate on the way through, the clubface will stay open and the ball will miss its intended target to the right. To play consistently using this rotation of the forearm, one must hit thousands of balls daily to perfect this. Not many of us have that kind of time to practice.

Just getting the club to eight o'clock can be difficult the first few times. One common fault I see students make in the trying to place or force the club to exactly eight o'clock. By doing this, the student becomes more mechanical and tense. The swing also has no flow to it. As your hips rotate, just let the shoulders, arms and club move and swing through the eight o'clock position. The arms just swing back and react to what the hips and shoulders do and get to where they are supposed to as a result.

I have seen many mistakes made in the takeaway. If you do not get it right the first time, do not get discouraged. It takes time, practice and patience. Changes never come easily or overnight. For every change you make in your swing, it will take about three to four weeks to become comfortable with that change and about three months to make that change a habit. Everybody is different in this. Some students take more or less time for the changes to take effect. Part of the reason is everyone learns at a different rate. The rest has to do on how much practice they do and how they practice. If your goal is to improve, you must put in time on the range and practice. This goes for all aspects of the game. The golf swing is really only a small portion of the game. The short game is the large portion.

Another one of the more common faults I have come across is the tendency to literally shift one's weight to the right side on the backswing and then shift back to the left on the downswing. There's nothing wrong with doing this but there are a few inconsistencies. For example, when the hips move laterally, there is a lack of coil with the upper body. With no coil, there's very little power stored up in the backswing. The problem with the hips moving laterally is you must get the hands more involved in the golf swing than they need to be. As the hips move forward laterally (sliding), the right shoulder works down towards the right knee. This, in effect, causes the right arm to get trapped against the right side of your body. Now you are forced to rotate or flip the hands over in order to square off the club. For the ball to fly to its intended target, the timing must be absolutely perfect. It is very hard to be that precise no matter how many balls you hit a day. I have seen very few amateurs or professionals who use a lot of hand rotation in their swing and play consistently. With the hips sliding forward the upper body does not have the support of the right leg to rotate on top of. Therefore, the hands must come into play, otherwise the ball will not fly to its intended target.

The weight shift is one of those things that will happen as a result of having proper body rotation and good fundamentals. It is not created or produced. When trying to force or produce the weight shift, you create unnecessary and wasted motion that has very little power to it. I have seen many students shift their weight by sliding the hips back in the backswing and then slide them forward in the downswing and through impact. Remember what I said earlier, "the more you do or more motion you create, the less you'll get out of it, but the less motion you have, the more consistent and accurate you'll be."

Chapter 6: Position Two – The Top

To get to the second position, the club must go up. Why? Well, what goes up must come down. Getting the club to go up is a fairly simple process. Let's just walk through the swing in slow motion to get a feel as to how the club makes its way to the top. Once you get the club to eight o'clock, bend your right arm until you form a 90 degree angle between the right forearm and the bicep and keep your left arm fairly straight but not locked. Make sure you complete your upper body rotation as you bend the right arm. Your shoulders should be about 90 degrees at the top of the swing. You should also feel pressure in your right hamstring.

At the top of the swing, you want the club to be just short of parallel to the ground with the irons. The woods will be about parallel to the ground. If the club is well past parallel, check to see if your right or left arm is bent too much. The shorter, more compact swing is more powerful and consistent than the longer swing. In the longer swing, the wrists and, or the arms break or hinge more. Should the wrists hinge too much, the pad of the left hand tends to come off the club. This means that in the downswing, they will have to move more also. Why? Simply put, for every action, there is a reaction. For every extra move made in the backswing, you'll need another extra move in the downswing to compensate for errors made in the backswing. The compensations tend to be instinctive and are not thought of in the swing. The golf swing happens to fast and you don't have time to actually think of making the necessary adjustment. Even making an adjustment in the downswing usually will result in a poor shot.

Some positive aspects of a short swing include more control, consistency in shots, more power, less effort and miss hits are not as bad. Having more control over the hands and arms through the rotation of the body is important. While the rotation of the upper body moves the arms and club, the speed of the arms and clubhead are controlled. The tempo of the swing also gets much smoother because the upper body is controlling or dictating the speed of the arms and club. With this happening, you'll feel like the arms and club move much slower in the downswing, but you gain more consistent clubhead speed. This in effect can give you more distance. More importantly, you see more consistent distance, trajectory and accuracy. All of these aspects work jointly together and have been explained in previous chapters.

So what about the long swing? In most instances, the long swing breaks down in different areas for golfers. No two golfers swing alike because of different body types. The fundamentals are still the same though. With a long swing, the arms have a tendency to bend more, which I covered earlier. In some golfers, the angle of the spine can tilt to the left at the top of the golf swing causing a long swing but at the same time they could retain the angles of the arms. In this instance the weight is on the left side and the golfer will have to either shift his weight back to the right side on the downswing or keep the weight on the left side. By having to shift the weight back to the right side on the downswing, it will be difficult to shift the weight to the left because of the lack of momentum needed to get there. Also, there is no coiling of the upper body to give you that unwinding or momentum to get the back to the left side. By keeping the weight on the left side at the start of the downswing, the club will come down on a steeper swing plane. Therefore you'll be hitting more down on the ball and getting a much lower ball flight with very little power behind it. You can also hit down so steeply on the ball to pop it up in the air because you're hitting the ball on the upper groves of the club with a driver.

How do we know if the club is square and in the proper position at the top? One of the first things I'll look for at the top is the clubface in relation to the left forearm. Once the student is at the top, the leading edge of the clubface should be parallel to the left forearm or close to it to be square. If the leading edge of the clubface is perpendicular to the ground, then it is open. Should the leading edge of the clubface be facing more towards the sky, it is in a closed position. You can play from either of these positions at the top, but there will have to be a compensation made in the downswing to get the club back to square at impact if the clubface is in either a closed or open position.

Another part of the top of the swing I look at is the positioning of the arms. The left arm should be fairly straight, while the right forearm should be bent no more than 90 degrees and be in a line parallel to the spine angle. The right forearm must also stay in front of your chest and not get behind your shoulder turn. The right arm getting behind the shoulder turn is one of the more common flaws I see students make at the top of the golf swing. If the right arm gets behind your shoulder turn, it may get caught behind the hip as you try to rotate through the ball. This will cause you to hit the ball to the right, or rotate the hands over to try to get the club square at impact. You could also hit behind the ball. Any numerous things can happen. Figure 3 and figure 4 are on the following pages.

Figure 3

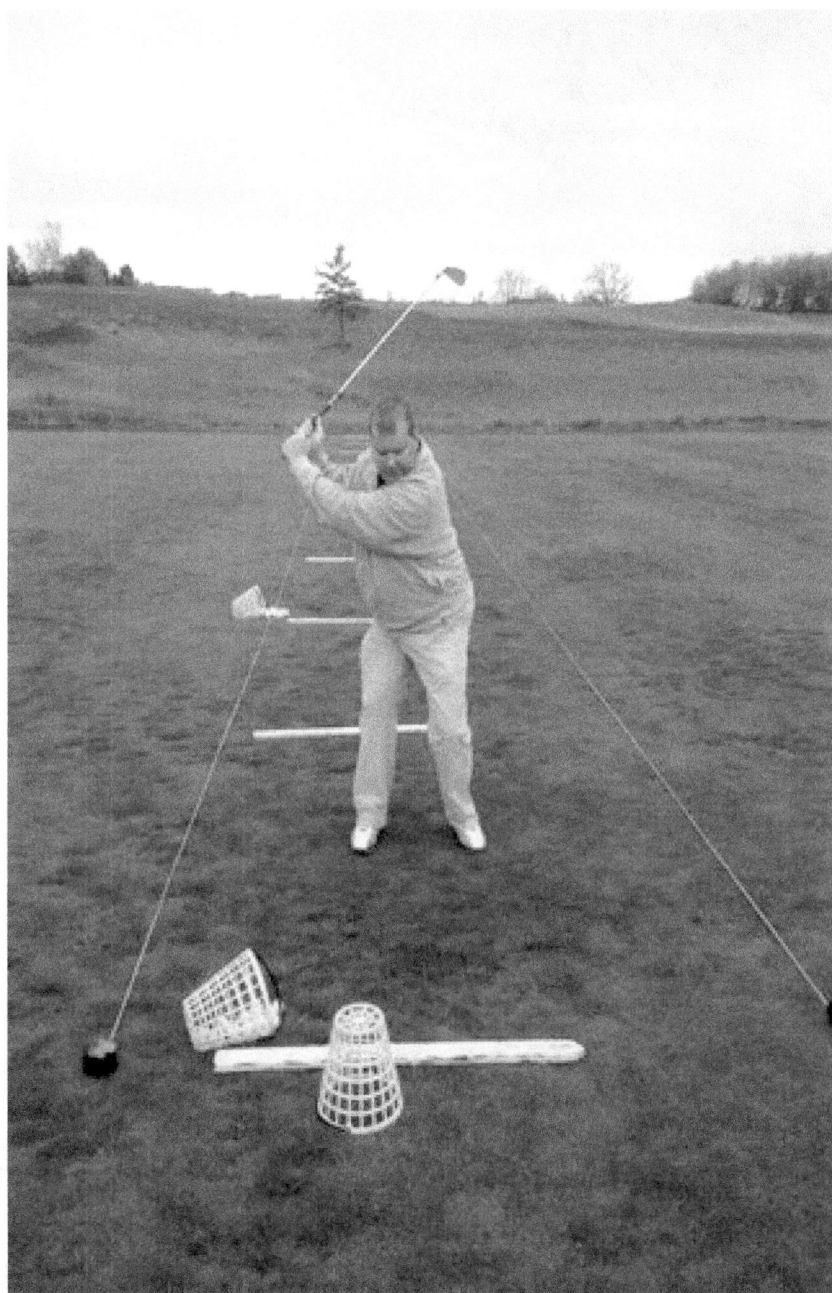

Figure 4

CHAPTER 7: POSITION THREE – IMPACT

Now that you know how the club goes back, how do you bring it down? As the club approaches the top of the swing, you want to feel a slight hesitation. This hesitation is actually the start of the downswing. What actually happens at this point is a change in the direction of the club. The reason for the hesitation or pause at the top is that your body is going in two different directions at the same time. As the arms and shoulders approach the top of the swing, your left leg should start to move back to its original starting position, thus starting the downswing. This is called the transition.

There are different ways on how to start the downswing. Many golf instructors favor starting the downswing with the legs. While this is correct, many golfers have a hard time with this. I have found that students who have been trying this usually have a flaw either during transition or just after. In most cases, the student starts the left leg back to its original starting position and allows the left knee to continue past that point. This in turn causes the hips to react by sliding forward, which in turn can cause the right shoulder to work down towards a point behind the ball. As a result, the hands will have to rotate over to get the clubface back to square at impact or the clubface will remain open producing a shot to the right of the target. Thus, relying on timing the hands to square the clubface off to get the ball to its intended target. As you can see, one breakdown can cause many others and allow for excess and/or wasted motion. The golf swing is very simple, so why complicate matters with excess. The key to having a successful swing is simplicity.

Other instructors favor starting the downswing with the left hip. Again, as a THOUGHT this is fine. Actually trying to start with the hip could cause some of the same scenarios as above. Although there is nothing wrong with starting your left hip to start your downswing. I like to use that as a swing thought when I feel my hips are not working properly.

Too much focus seems to be put on the making or forcing the downswing in getting in the exact right position. Positions are nothing more than reference points used when looking at the swing from a static position or looking at video of your golf swing. As I said earlier, they are not exact, only points of reference. From a dynamic motion, the club or body passes through these reference points but again are not exact. Remember what I said earlier, the golf swing is a reaction to a target that you have in your mind's eye. It is the same with the downswing. The transition is a reaction. By putting the focus on other areas, students achieve the transition through reaction.

So how do you start this process? I like to start by focusing on the right side during the downswing. Many may disagree with this, but I've had great success with this in students. To first understand this, we must work through it mechanically and in pieces. Remember, you want things to react by putting the focus on a different area.

As you walk through the swing, take notice on how the rest of your body will start to REACT to certain movements. The simplest way to start the downswing is to allow the right arm to unfold, but do not let your wrists break or unhinge. The lag in the wrists must be maintained. You want to use the right arm more like a lever, just like when you hammer a nail but without breaking the wrists. As the right arm unfolds the hands should come down towards the right knee or foot until the shaft of the club reaches parallel to the ground. Do not worry about the moving the legs. They will move by reacting to what your arms are doing. You should feel as though hands and arms are dropping with no resistance. Gravity wants to naturally pull your arms and club down. Why try to resist? Let gravity do its job. Now, notice what has happened to your legs as you brought the club down. Your left leg should have gone back to its original starting position and may have started to even straighten up a little. Once the club is at parallel to the ground, turn your right hip and shoulders through and allow the arms to be pulled through the ball. See figure 6 and figure 7 on the following pages..

Figure 6

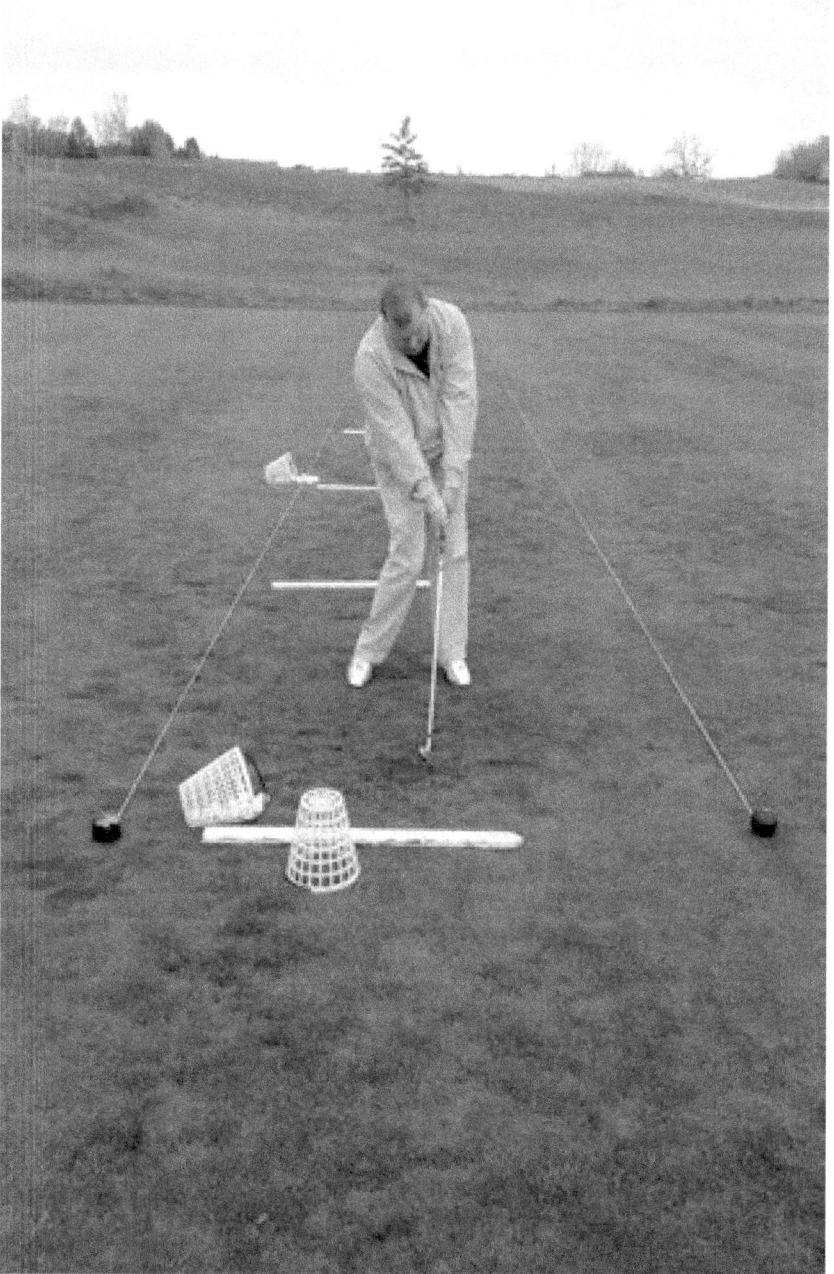

Figure 7

It may feel like your arms are staying behind the rotation of your body a little. Do not try to add any speed with the arms as you do this. It will can cause you to either miss hit the ball or hit the ball using your arms and not your body. If you try to add speed by swinging the arms faster, your body will not be able to keep up. Everything has to move together as a unit and have good tempo. If everything works together the swing becomes easy, but when working as individual parts the results can be very bad.

With good fundamentals, the golf swing can become a reaction and just happen with little or no thought. You should not be thinking of your golf swing while standing over the ball. That should be left at the range. When on the course, the body does nothing more than react to the target you see in your mind's eye. Impossible? No. Take, for example, the act of catching a ball. Have someone throw a ball to you. Now try to explain how you caught the ball. The answer is not you just stuck out your hand. Explain the mechanics of how you actually caught the ball. Kind of hard isn't it. Did you think of exactly where you had to place your hand and the position it must be in for you to catch the ball? No. You didn't think you more reacted. It is the same thing with the golf swing. You react to the target you see in your mind's eye and allow the body to react. What could be simpler. By working and reinforcing your basic fundamentals, this is possible.

A common fault I find students make in the downswing is they pull the right elbow into their side. This traps the arm and as a result the body can't square the club off at impact. The only thing left to do is to rotate the hands and forearms to square off the club. Also, because the elbow has been pulled into the side, the club can decelerate. This happens because the right arm does not work like a lever. I've talked about this earlier in this chapter. With deceleration of the club, comes a lack of distance, fat shots and hitting behind the ball, just to name a few things that could result from this.

Another flaw I find students making in the downswing is trying to get the left hip to clear. In most instances, students will spin the hip instead of rotating the hip. This can lead to trapping the right elbow into the side also just like above. The hips do not have far to rotate compared to the rest of the body. Let the hips, shoulders and arms move together as unit and you'll have much more success.

Now comes the final part of the swing, the follow through or finish. It is nothing more than a mirror image of your backswing. What do I mean? Simply put, what you do on the backswing, you do the same as the follow through. The momentum on the downswing is what allows the club to finish where it does. If you decelerate, the swing does not get finished because there is not enough speed or momentum to carry you through to the finish. Once you get the club through impact, allow your arms to simply fold or bend in an upward direction and your hands will finish over the left shoulder. The shaft of the club should be across the back of your neck or across the shoulders. A drill I like to use with students is to have them get an image of a bell being in front of them and about ten feet off the ground. As they swing through the ball try hitting the imaginary bell with the clubhead. The only way to do this is to allow the club to go up by bending the arms. This is how we finish the swing. If the club swings around your body, the club won't go up and hit the imaginary bell.

Chapter 8: Golf Course Management

Until recently, golf course management has been an area that has not written about enough. You could write an entire book on this subject alone, but for now, a brief summary will be sufficient for the beginner to the better than average golfer.

What exactly is course management? It is the ability to maneuver the ball through the golf course and put your ball in the best possible position on each hole to get the ball in the hole in the least number of strokes. Sounds complicated and a lot of thinking involved. How does one accomplish this? Does this mean you must hit driver on every par four and par five? Not necessarily. One thing is certain, you must play within your ability and never try to execute a shot you have not practiced, not hit before, or had no success in the past pulling it off or have no confidence in. For example, if a shot calls for you to hook the ball around a bend, and you have never hit a hook before, what do you do? Many would try to hit the hook and not succeed and leave them in a bad position or in trouble. This could cost you more strokes. The smart play would be to hit your shot past the bend leaving you a clear shot to the green. This avoids getting into any trouble that could have resulted in trying to hit the hook shot and in the long run save you strokes.

Course management is basically common sense and not allowing your EGO to get in the way. It is mainly choosing the right club to hit from tee to fairway to help set yourself up too get to the green. Choosing what club, type of shot and where on the green to hit the ball to depends on a few factors. Determining what club to hit off the tee depends largely on distance to the hole (i.e. 395 yards), wind direction and shape of the hole. When looking at the shape of a hole, look for sand trap placement if any, creeks, ponds, hazards, out of bounds, width of fairway, dogleg left or right or straight away. Let's take, for example, a hole that's 395 yards long with a 25 yard width fairway. Add in an out of bounds on the right side and a sand trap on the left side of the fairway about 210 yards out and a 10 mile an hour wind left to right. What do you hit? I like have students play backwards from green to tee. By learning to play this way, you want to ask yourself "what club do I want to hit into the green." Let's say you want to hit an 7 iron in to the green and you can hit the nine iron 150 yards. Now subtract 150 yards from the distance of the hole 395, result of 245 yards. Now pick the club that you can hit 245 yards. Say that's your driver. Now look at the shape of the hole. Do you tend to hit the ball to the right? If you do you may want to hit a three wood off the tee to keep the ball in play, especially with out of bounds to the right and a somewhat narrow fairway. The object is to keep the ball in play and avoid unnecessary penalty strokes on this particular hole. By hitting a three wood, you'll have to hit maybe a six or seven iron into the green but you will have succeeded in avoiding a bunker and out of bounds. As far as the wind goes, aim a little bit farther left leaving room for the wind to push the ball to the right a little. You don't always need to hit driver. On short par fours many times it is beneficial to hit a wood or hybrid off the tee to keep the ball in play. It also helps to avoid hitting a finesse wedge or taking a half swing if you get to close to the green.

It is the tee shot that sets us up to get into a position to score well. Patience here is a must but delivery is everything. It can make us or break us.

On par fives, take 3 to 4 swings to get to the green if you

do not hit the ball very far. You can still make par by making a putt if on the green in 4 strokes. The main key to course management is to keep the ball in play and avoid wasting shots. It is a lot easier to take your lumps when you have a bad hole and play for bogey or double bogey than trying to pull off a high risk high reward shot that can cost you more strokes than necessary. You have plenty of holes to make up for that one bad hole you just had.

CHAPTER 9: GOLF PSYCHOLOGY

Golf is more mental at any level more so than most sports. In most sports, you or the ball is always in motion. You don't have time to think, only react. With golf, we have to start from a static position or non moving position. This gives us too much time to think about what we are going to do instead of just reacting.

Golf is a game that is 80% mental for the average player and 100% mental for the low handicapper and professionals. How is it very mental you may ask? The simplest way to explain this is to give you any example. Let's take for our example a 150 yard par three with a water hazard from the front of the tee to 10 yards short of the green. After choosing your club, what do you start to think about or what is going through your mind? If you are thinking about not putting the ball in the water hazard, chances are you will find your ball at the bottom of the water hazard. Why you may ask? The answer is very simple. Look at the phrase "not putting the ball in the water." Notice the term "not." The way the mind works psychologically is that it does not understand negative terms such as not, can't, don't etc. What the mind does understand is everything after the word not. The mind only picks up "putting the ball in to the water." So what happens most of the time when thinking in this way is you hit the ball in to the water hazard and may not understand why you do this when you told yourself not to.

When you think in terms of language or words to communicate what you want the body to do, the mind can send mixed signals to the body through the nervous system to do what you don't want to do. In other words, it gets confused. In this example of not putting a ball in the water, most students I've taught over the years have said their thought process or sole thought was to not put the ball in the water. Most of the time, they put the ball in the water. By simply changing their thought process onto a positive thought, such as seeing the ball land in the fairway in their mind, the results went the other way. The student then starts to get the ball over the water more often and in the end gains more confidence. The point to all this is elementary. Visualizing the shot or what you are trying to accomplish has more positive results and also sends clearer messages to the body than words.

Anytime you think negatively, the result will usually be exactly what you were trying to avoid doing. How do you work on the mental side of the game? Simple. Always try to focus on the shot you want to hit and not what you do not want to hit. On the golf course, as well as in practice, one should always thing of positive shots and have confidence you will hit the shot. Secondly, never try to hit a shot you have never practiced or succeeded in pulling off before. The chances of hitting a shot you've never hit or practiced are slim to none and will cost you more shots than simple playing it safe. Even with good visualization of the shot and knowing how to hit it, the odds are slim at best, if you've never hit the shot or practiced it.

A good friend of mine once told me early in my professional career as a player, when in trouble, whether it be off the tee or your approach shot, accept it and play for bogey or double bogey, depending on your type of game. Often times you'll be surprised by the end result. When I started to do that, playing for bogey when I got into trouble, many times I ended up walking away with a par and sometimes a birdie. How can that be? I think part of the reason for this is I took the pressure of forcing myself to make a par and accepted bogey. In the end, I was more relaxed and let things more happen instead of trying to force it and get worked up. This in part is how you start to score better and enjoy the game more.

There is a lot more I could talk about for the mental aspect of the game. I haven't even scratched the surface. My hope is to give you a little insight to the mental part of the game without getting to technical.

My philosophy is to keep the golf swing and the mental part of it as simple as I can. I like to get students to learn to think differently and at the same time focus on where they want the ball to go, not the mechanics of the swing while playing a round of golf. Only then can you enjoy the game.

A FINAL WORD

Hopefully after reading this book, you'll have gained a better understanding of the golf swing and how to play the game itself through better course management. One thing you may understand about the game of golf is that it is a lot like life itself. There are always new challenges and hurtles to get over. Golf is one of those games that is a never ending learning process. Nobody knows everything there is to know about the golf swing, but with changing technology, we are always researching the swing to further our understanding and learn how to keep it simple. Simplicity is the real key to the enjoyment of the game itself

Through physics, geometry, biomechanics, anatomy, bone structure, and psychology we learn how the body can move in the most efficient way to create the most amount of power with the simplest motion and the least amount of work. The less you have to do in the swing, the more you'll get out of it. Simplicity is the key.

Golf is a game to be played and enjoyed. It will have its up and downs, good days and bad. When it comes time to play the game, forget thinking about how to swing the club and focus your mind on the target at hand. This is the game. Golf is a target game. Focus on hitting your target with each swing. You'll have much more fun and may even find the game becomes easier. As Shivas Irons once said, "take time to look at the scenery and smell the fresh air and flowers." You may find more enjoyment and relaxation in the game and in your surroundings, which we sometimes take for granted.

Always try to remember the good shots you have had and try to forget the bad ones. I know, easier said than done. The final thought is about negativity. It is the fastest way to destroy a round for the morning or afternoon depending on when one plays.

As for the final words, may your ball always find the short grass of the fairway and green and in the end the bottom of the cup.

ABOUT THE AUTHOR

Michael Callahan lives in East Aurora, New York with his three sons. He is a certified USGTF Teaching Professional and certified master club fitter. He boasts over 26 years of teaching experience within all levels from beginner to professional. For the last 4 years Michael has exhibited his talents at the Broadway Driving Range and Miniature Golf, in Depew, New York, where he created an admirable comprehensive golf learning center. Michael has a real passion for teaching fundamentals of the golf swing and enjoys witnessing the transformation of his students to inspired golfers.

www.ingramcontent.com/pod-product-compliance
Lightning Source LLC
LaVergne TN
LVHW021544080426
835509LV00019B/2828